KANGAROOS

Jolyon Goddard

Grolier
an imprint of

SCHOLASTIC
www.scholastic.com/librarypublishing

Published 2009 by Grolier
An imprint of Scholastic Library Publishing
Old Sherman Turnpike, Danbury,
Connecticut 06816

For The Brown Reference Group plc
Project Editor: Jolyon Goddard
Picture Researcher: Clare Newman
Designers: Dave Allen, Jeni Child, Lynne Ross,
          Sarah Williams
Managing Editors: Bridget Giles, Tim Harris

Volume ISBN-13: 978-0-7172-6298-4
Volume ISBN-10: 0-7172-6298-7

Library of Congress
Cataloging-in-Publication Data

Nature's children. Set 4.
    p. cm.
  Includes bibliographical references and
  index.
  ISBN 13: 978-0-7172-8083-4
  ISBN 10: 0-7172-8083-7 ((set 4) : alk. paper)
  1. Animals--Encyclopedias, Juvenile. 1.
  Grolier (Firm)
  QL49.N385 2009
  590.3--dc22
                        2007046315

Printed and bound in China

PICTURE CREDITS

Front Cover: **FLPA**: Gerard Lacz.

Back Cover: **FLPA**: Gerard Lacz, Mitsuaki
Iwago/Minden Pictures; **Shutterstock**:
Anna Dzondzua, Sharon D.

FLPA: Gerry Ellis 22, Mitsuaki Iwago/Minden
Pictures 41, 42, Jurgen and Christine Sohn
21; **Nature PL**: Thomas Lazar 9, Owen
Newman 37, Staffan Widstrand 26–27;
Photolibrary.com: Himani 29, Belinda
Wright 17; **Shutterstock**: Bruce Amos 2–3,
Mark Bonham 45, cbpix 14, Susan Flashman
18, Eric Gevaert 33, Jan Gorlwald 13, Damir
Karan 4, Timothy Craig Lubcke 30, Phil
Morley 34, Styve Reineck 46, Timbles 6, M.
Willis 10, WizData, Inc 5; **Still Pictures**:
Dave Watts/BIOS 38.

Contents

FACT FILE: Kangaroos

Class	Mammals (Mammalia)
Order	Cuscuses, possum, koalas, wombats, and kangaroos (Diprotodontia)
Families	Kangaroos, wallaroos, and wallabies (Macropodidae); rat kangaroos, bettongs, and potoroos (Potoroidae); and the musky rat kangaroo (Hypsiprymnodontidae)
Genera	16 genera
Species	76 species
World distribution	Australia, New Guinea, and small islands in that region
Habitat	Varies with species
Distinctive physical characteristics	Deerlike or ratlike head; most kangaroos have small front legs, large back legs, and a large tail; fur might be shades of red, brown, or gray; females have a pouch on belly
Habits	Many live in groups; most travel around by hopping; females raise young in their pouch
Diet	Most eat grass; some eat insects and worms

4

Introduction

Kangaroos are among the most recognizable of all **mammals**. Red kangaroos, gray kangaroos, and wallabies are familiar to most people. However, there are many other types of kangaroos, including wallaroos, bettongs, potoroos, and rat kangaroos. In fact, there are 76 **species**, or types, of kangaroos. Although they come in a range of sizes and fur colors, many kangaroos look similar. Most have a deerlike or ratlike head, large ears, short front legs, large back legs for hopping around, and a long tail for balance. In addition, an adult female kangaroo often has a baby, or **joey**, poking its head out of the **pouch** on her belly.

Although a symbol of Australia, kangaroos are often seen as pests, especially by farmers.

The females of most types of marsupials have a pouch. A joey pokes its head out from its mother's pouch.

6

Pouched Mammals

Kangaroos are mammals. All mammals are warm-blooded animals with fur that feed their young on milk. Kangaroos are also **marsupials** (MAHR-SOO-PEE-ULZ). These are mammals that give birth to their young at an early stage of development. After being born, most young marsupials complete their development in a fold of stretchy skin, called a pouch, on their mother's belly.

At birth, most marsupials are about the size of a jellybean. Their eyes, back legs, and tail are undeveloped. All they can do is crawl with their surprisingly strong front legs into the pouch. There, they clamp onto a teat and **nurse**. They drink their mother's rich milk for several months, living in warmth and comfort.

Including kangaroos, there are more than 330 species of marsupials. Wombats, the koala, possum, opossum, and the Tasmanian devil are all marsupials.

History Lesson

Marsupials first appeared in what is now North America more than 80 million years ago. At that time, the continents were still attached to one another. The marsupials were able to spread into South America, Europe, North Africa, and Asia. They reached Australia, which at that time was attached to South America, about 60 million years ago.

As Australia slowly drifted away from South America, many new species of marsupials **evolved**, or developed gradually over millions of years, on the island. The marsupials in Australia were isolated, or alone. However, in other parts of the world, new types of mammals appeared. The marsupials outside Australia had to compete with these new animals. The new mammals included **predators** that ate marsupials, as well as other mammals better suited to their **habitats** than the marsupials. Eventually, all the marsupials outside Australia and its nearby islands went **extinct**, except for the opossum of North and South America.

Now too big for their mother's pouch, the young of a female common opossum from South America cling to her fur.

A young kangaroo searches for food on a beach.

Life Down Under

Kangaroos live in Australia, New Guinea, and islands surrounding these two countries. Some kangaroos have been brought by humans to New Zealand. There are even some wallabies living wild in a few parts of the United Kingdom—although many die during particularly severe winters.

Kangaroos have evolved to survive in many different habitats. The larger species prefer grasslands. Other kangaroos live in swamplands. Some species are found in forests—hopping around on the ground or climbing in the trees. A few types prefer to live on rocky hills or cliffs. Some kangaroos can even tough it out in Australia's deserts, which cover almost half of the continent.

Red Kangaroos

The largest kangaroo is the red kangaroo, which is found on the vast, dry grasslands that stretch across much of Australia. Male red kangaroos grow to almost 7 feet (2.1 m) high and weigh up to 200 pounds (90 kg). The males usually have reddish fur, but the females' fur is normally bluish-gray. In some regions, the females are red, and the males are gray! Females weigh less than the males and can hop faster—for this reason, Australians call the females "blue fliers."

During the **mating** season, the males produce a red powder from glands on their throat and chest. To attract the females, the males rub this substance over their fur, making it even redder.

Not only the largest kangaroo, the red kangaroo is also the largest of all marsupials.

This trio of eastern gray kangaroos includes a mother and her joey. The joey is still dependent on its mother, but it is now too big for her pouch.

Gray Kangaroos

Although red kangaroos are the tallest kangaroos, gray kangaroos are often heavier. That's because they have a stockier build. There are two species of gray kangaroos. The eastern gray kangaroo lives in the open forests near the east coast of Australia. Its fur is not always gray—sometimes it is brown—and its tail has a black tip. The western gray kangaroo lives near the west coast of Australia. Its coat is a muddy-gray color.

Like red kangaroos, grays mainly eat grass and low-growing plants. Gray kangaroos are quite vocal—they make a variety of different sounds, including growls, coughs, and clucks, to communicate with one another.

Wallaroos

A kangaroo that is smaller than red and gray kangaroos but bigger than a wallaby is called a wallaroo—a mixture of the words "kangaroo" and "wallaby." There are just two species of wallaroos—the hill wallaroo, or euro, and the smaller black wallaroo.

Wallaroos look similar to their larger relatives, but have shorter legs and a thicker-set body. Hill wallaroos are common in many parts of Australia. Black wallaroos are very shy and live only in northern Australia. Both species live in rocky landscapes and small boulder-strewn valleys. Their fur is shaggier than that of other kangaroos and varies from sandy yellow and bluish-gray to reddish-brown and black.

Wallaroos are tough kangaroos that are used to surviving in harsh conditions. They often hide in caves away from the heat of the sun. Wallaroos can survive without water for long periods of time—up to a month. But when they become really thirsty, they dig for water, sometimes up to 3 feet (90 cm) into the ground.

The male black wallaroo has very dark fur. Female black wallaroos have brown or gray fur.

17

The swamp wallaby lives along the eastern coast of Australia. It has a strong odor, which gives the anima its other name—the stinker

Wallabies

Smaller than wallaroos, wallabies range from 4 to 50 pounds (1.8 to 22 kg) in weight. There are many types of wallabies—about 45 different species in all—and they are all very unique. Some types live in groups, others live alone. Many are closely related to the larger kangaroos. They look like smaller versions of the large kangaroos. The agile wallaby, the red-necked wallaby, the Parma wallaby, and the pretty-faced wallaby, which has distinctive markings on its face, are all closely related to the large kangaroos.

Rock wallabies live in caves and have feet suited for hopping around steep hills and cliffs. Hare wallabies are about the same size as a hare and can bound away very quickly at the first sign of danger. Nail-tailed wallabies have a horny growth like a fingernail at the end of their tail. Other wallabies include the curiously named pademelons (PA-DUH-MEH-LUNZ), dorcopsises (DOR-KOP-SEE-SIZ), and the quokka.

Tree Kangaroos

Tree kangaroos are suited to climbing trees. Therefore, their body is somewhat different from the body of kangaroos that live on the ground. Their front and back legs are about the same size. They have long claws, especially on their front legs, that grip well. The undersides of their paws have rough, soft pads that prevent the animal from slipping on branches. The tree kangaroo's long furry tail helps it balance when climbing and jumping among branches. This kangaroo can jump long distances, and it has even been known to jump from heights of 50 feet (18 m) to the ground below. On the ground, the tree kangaroo hops like other kangaroos—but somewhat awkwardly.

Tree kangaroos live high up in the trees of rain forests. They eat leaves and fruit. At night, they venture down to the ground to eat plants that are an essential part of their diet. If any predators appear, the tree kangaroos scurry back up a tree trunk. In the 1990s, two new species of tree kangaroos were discovered in New Guinea.

There are 12 species of tree
kangaroos, including this
rare Huon (HYOO-on) tree
kangaroo. Tree kangaroos live
in the mountainous forests of
northeastern Australia, New
Guinea, and nearby islands.

The brush-tailed bettong of southwestern Australia is a type of rat kangaroo. Once widespread, the animal is now rare due to predation and habitat loss.

Rat Kangaroos

The smallest types of kangaroos are the least kangaroo-like of the kangaroos. There are about ten different species of these small rat kangaroos. The biggest rat kangaroo is about the size of a rabbit, and the smallest is the size of a rat. They live mainly in forests and coastal areas. Unlike most other kangaroos, which eat grass and leaves, rat kangaroos prefer roots, insects, fungi, and worms. These kangaroos are active at night and sleep during the day. Some gather grass with their tail to make a nest in which they sleep. One type of rat kangaroo, called the boodie, or burrowing bettong, sleeps in an underground **burrow** in sand dunes.

Most rat kangaroos hop around on their back legs like their larger relatives. However, the musky rat kangaroo, which is the smallest of the rat kangaroos, runs around on all fours. This rat kangaroo, has five toes on each foot—other kangaroos have four toes. It also has a scaly, hairless tail unlike other kangaroos.

On the Hop

Kangaroos do not run like other animals. Instead, they bounce, or hop, along on their powerful back legs, with their long tail helping them stay balanced. Big kangaroos usually hop along at a steady pace of about 12 miles (20 km) per hour. However, they can go twice as fast as that in short bursts, especially if they are being chased by a predator. At such times, a big kangaroo might leap 25 feet (8 m) with each bound! They can jump as high as 10 feet (3 m), but usually they only leap half this height.

The secret of a kangaroo's hopping success is the muscles and **tendons** in its back legs. Tendons are like large elastic bands that join muscles to bones. As a kangaroo lands after each hop, the legs bend and the tendon in each leg is stretched. As that happens, the leg muscles shorten. The stretched tendon then springs back to its original length and the muscle loosens. That pushes the kangaroo forward into another leap. Kangaroos do not always hop. Sometimes they move slowly on all fours, especially when they are **grazing**.

Big Feet

Scientists call all kangaroos, except the rat kangaroos, macropods. The word *macropod* is Greek for "big foot." Some kangaroos have feet that are 18 inches (45 cm) long. When standing, a kangaroo rests on its large feet and tail—like a tripod.

Almost all kangaroos have four toes on their feet. A kangaroo's second and third toes are joined together. The fourth toe is the biggest and strongest toe. It provides most of the support for the kangaroo's body.

A kangaroo's front paws have five fingers. The front paws are much, much smaller than the back feet. The kangaroo cannot grip very well with its front paws. It uses them to scratch itself, for support when moving slowly, for fighting, and for picking at food on the ground.

On land, a kangaroo's back legs do not move separately, so it can only hop and not walk. However, when swimming, the back legs can move independently.

In the Mob

A group of kangaroos is called a **mob**. There are usually between 10 and 20 members in a mob. The mob is led by the strongest member, which is often the biggest male. This kangaroo is sometimes called the "old man." Male kangaroos are called **boomers**, and females are called **does**. Each mob contains a mixture of boomers, does, and young.

Members of the mob come and go. Some stay a few days before wandering off, others spend years in the same mob. The strongest bond is between the does and their joeys. Mobs move around in the wild, in search of food and water. Most kangaroos prefer to feed at night, when it is cooler. However, they will feed during the day in the winter months. Often, different mobs come together to graze peacefully in the same location.

All eyes and ears—the kangaroos in this mob are distracted from their grazing.

Germs inside a kangaroo's stomach help the animal break down tough plant matter. This allows the kangaroo to obtain as many nutrients from its food as possible.

A Lot of Chewing

Kangaroos mainly eat grass. However, they will also munch on other low-growing plants and sometimes reach up for leaves on trees. Many kangaroos prefer dry and coarse grass to the soft green type of grass that grows on lawns. Their sharp front teeth, which stick out, snip like scissors at tough vegetation.

Many kangaroos chew their food for a long time. Large back teeth, called molars, grind plant matter into a fine pulp before it is swallowed. The food then spends a long time in the kangaroo's large stomach, where it is **digested**, or broken down, further. That allows the kangaroo to get the maximum nutrition out of its food. Some kangaroos, like many other grazers, such as cows, deer, and antelope, do not digest their food in one go. They swallow their food and then bring it back up to chew it further, usually when they are resting. This double-chewing is known as "chewing the cud."

Kangaroos also need to drink plenty of water, so they tend to feed near water holes or streams.

On the Lookout

Kangaroos are always on the alert. It's very difficult to sneak up on them. They are naturally nervous and shy, and they never seem to be able to relax completely. Even when kangaroos are asleep, the slightest rustle will wake them. They sleep for only short periods of time, and frequently get up to check for any danger.

Kangaroos have sharp senses. Their large brown eyes can see far into the distance. They have good night vision, too. Their ears, which can turn toward the source of a sound, are very sharp. Kangaroos also have a highly developed sense of smell.

Gray kangaroos, like this one below, have a hairy nose. Other kangaroos have a less hairy or hairless nose.

Licking the fur helps
keep it clean. It also
cools the kangaroo as
the saliva evaporates.

Keeping Clean

Like most other mammals, kangaroos spend a lot of time keeping their fur in tiptop condition. The kangaroo **grooms**, or cleans, its fur much like a pet cat does. It licks one of its front paws and rubs it on its face and fur to clean itself, brush away dirt, and smooth down the fur. Kangaroos also groom themselves with their back feet. They use the two claws on their joined second and third toes like tweezers to pick out **parasites** in the fur. Parasites—such as ticks and fleas—live in a kangaroo's fur. These pests bite the kangaroo's skin to feed on blood.

Female kangaroos, or does, groom their joeys with their tongue. Smaller types of kangaroos sometimes clean their fur by swimming in rivers or lakes.

Boxing Boomers

Kangaroos are usually gentle. However, that can change if two boomers are interested in mating with the same does, or if the "old man" is challenged for leadership of the mob by a younger male. To settle the disagreement, boomers fight by boxing and kicking!

The old man and his challenger size each other up. They strut toward each other. Standing up to their full height, they then throw punches with their front paws. The fight heats up as the boomers lean back on their tails, lashing out with their powerful legs. They try to avoid each other's sharp claws. Sometimes, one fighter picks up the other in his front legs and throws him across the ground. One boomer will eventually tire and back down. There may be a few injuries, but those are likely to be just scratches—kangaroos have thick fur and very tough skin.

During a fight, a boomer supports itself using just its sturdy tail as it kicks its opponent.

A Tasmanian devil—the
largest living meat-eating
marsupial—makes a meal
of a wallaby.

Enemies!

Many animals eat kangaroos, especially joeys, if given the chance. Predators of kangaroos include snakes, large lizards, and eagles.

Thousands of years ago, kangaroo-eating marsupials roamed mainland Australia. These included the Tasmanian devil and the thylacine (THI-LUH-SEEN). Thylacines are now extinct—the last known one died in 1939 in a zoo in Tasmania, an island off the southern coast of Australia. Tasmanian devils now live only in Tasmania.

Now kangaroos' main enemy—except for humans—is the dingo. These dogs originally came to Australia with the first human settlers and now live in the wild. If a kangaroo spots a dingo, it might alert the others in the mob by stamping its foot or by giving a warning call. The kangaroos usually run away. If cornered, a kangaroo will defend itself by kicking and scratching with its sharp toe claws. A well-aimed kick from a big kangaroo can kill a dingo.

Getting Together

When a male kangaroo wants to mate with a female, he follows her around making clucking noises. He might even grab her tail to make his intentions very clear. He will court her anywhere between a couple of days and two weeks. After mating, the pair separates. The father does not help bring up his joeys.

In a mob of kangaroos, usually only the old man mates with the does. He fights off any rivals with a boxing and kicking match. That way, the does know that their joeys will be strong and healthy like their father.

Gray kangaroos can mate at any time of the year, although most joeys are born in summer.

After being born, it
takes the joey about
two minutes to crawl
into the pouch.

42

A Joey's Journey

A joey is born about a month after mating. Most kangaroos have just one baby, although sometimes twins are born, especially to musky rat kangaroos.

The doe gives her pouch a spring cleaning before she gives birth. A newborn kangaroo is blind, hairless, and tiny, weighing $\frac{1}{30}$ of an ounce (0.8 g) or less. It is born outside the pouch. It must find its own way to the pouch, dragging itself along with its front legs. The joey follows a trail of **mucus** that its mother has licked to the opening of the pouch. Once the joey is inside the pouch, it attaches itself to one of its mother's teats. Feeding on the warm, nourishing milk, the joey continues its development in the pouch.

Pouch Life

The joey remains in its mother's pouch for several months. In the dark and cozy pouch, the joey's eyes, ears, back legs, and tail develop. It also grows fur. At about five months old, the joey pokes its head out of the pouch for the first time to take a look at the outside world.

When the joey eventually emerges from the pouch to test its legs, its mother makes sure that it doesn't wander too far. Some joeys need a bit of prodding to come out. The doe has to bend forward to tip it out. The joey returns to the pouch every so often for comfort. Male and female joeys are the same size when they first leave the pouch. However, males then begin to grow faster and become bigger. Most adult male kangaroos are twice the size of the females.

A joey doesn't always have to leave the cozy warmth of its mother's pouch to nibble grass.

45

Large kangaroos live to about 15 years in the wild. In captivity they might reach 20 years. Smaller species live for about half as long.

Moving On

As a joey begins to spend time outside the pouch, it always stays near its mother. If there is any danger, it jumps back into the pouch. It usually dives in headfirst, and has to turn itself around in order to poke its head out.

Joeys love to play with other joeys. Sometimes, they play-fight and wrestle. These activities help develop the skills that they will need later in life to fight off predators or—in the case of males—become the leader of a mob. The pouch expands as the young kangaroo grows, but by ten months the joey is too big to fit it comfortably. The joey still stays close to its mother, but she prevents it from trying to get back in the pouch. By this time, the doe is ready to give birth to another joey.

At two and a half years, females are ready to have joeys of their own. The females of large kangaroos usually remain in the mob into which they were born. But the males eventually leave, hoping one day to lead their own mob.

Under Threat

Aborigines, the native people of Australia, hunted kangaroos for their meat and skin. They never killed more kangaroos than they needed. When European settlers arrived in Australia in the 18th century and onward, they began to change the landscape. They created fields for crops and pasture for cows and sheep. When people chopped down forests, many types of kangaroos lost their habitat. Smaller kangaroos were also threatened by animals, such as cats and foxes, that came with the settlers. Since European settlers arrived, four species of kangaroos have gone extinct.

Other kangaroos benefited by grazing on the pasture and crops. However, farmers saw them as pests and many thousands were shot. Today, there are strict controls on how many kangaroos can be killed each year.

The larger kangaroos are no longer under threat. Many of the smaller ones are now rare. However, there are now many nature **reserves** in Australia in which these rarer kangaroos are protected, offering hope for their future.

Words to Know

Aborigines	Native people of Australia.
Boomers	Male kangaroos.
Burrow	An animal's underground home.
Digested	When food is broken down in the body to extract its nutrients.
Does	Female kangaroos.
Evolved	Developed or changed gradually over many generations and thousands of years.
Extinct	When all of a certain type of animal or plant is dead and gone forever.
Grazing	Eating grass.
Grooms	Cleans and combs fur.
Habitats	Types of places in which animals or plants live. Different habitats include forests, deserts, and lakes.
Joey	A baby kangaroo.
Mammals	Animals with fur that feed their young on milk.

49

Marsupials	Mammals whose young are born at an early stage and complete their development feeding on milk, in most cases in their mother's pouch.
Mating	Coming together to produce young.
Mob	A group of kangaroos.
Mucus	A slimy substance produced by animals.
Nurse	To drink milk from the mother's body.
Parasites	Tiny animals that live on or in another animal's body, feeding on their body fluids or tissues.
Pouch	A stretchy fold of skin on a female kangaroo's belly in which its joey lives for several months.
Predators	Animals that hunt other animals.
Reserves	Areas of land in which animals and plants are protected.
Species	The scientific term for animals of the same type that breed together.
Tendons	Tough bands of tissue that attach muscles to bones inside an animal.

Find Out More

Books

Brust, B. W., D. Millsap, and J. B. Wexo. *Kangaroos.*
Zoobooks Series. Poway, California: Wildlife
Education, Ltd., 2001.

Montgomery, S. *Quest for the Tree Kangaroo: An Expedition
to the Cloud Forest of New Guinea.* Scientists in the Field.
Boston, Massachusetts: Houghton Mifflin, 2006.

Web sites

Kangaroo
*www.enchantedlearning.com/subjects/mammals/marsupial/
Kangaroocoloring.shtml*
Facts about kangaroos and a picture to print and color in.

Red Kangaroo
*animals.nationalgeographic.com/animals/mammals/
red-kangaroo.html*
A profile of the red kangaroo.

Index